RAMBLING

CU00763648

Darren Freebury-Jones is a lecturer in Shakespeare Studies in Stratford-upon-Avon, whose research on Shakespeare and his contemporaries can be found in a wide range of peer-reviewed journals and books. His work has been discussed in national newspapers such as *The Times, The Guardian, The Telegraph, The Observer,* and *The Independent.* He is also an actor and has spent much of his life writing fiction and poetry. He has a house in Cardiff, Wales, where he is from.

Also by Darren Freebury-Jones

Shakespeare's Borrowed Feathers	(Manchester University Press, 2024)
Shakespeare's Tutor	(Manchester University Press, 2022)
Reading Robert Greene	(Routledge, 2022)

Rambling

Darren Freebury-Jones

Broken Sleep Books

ISBN: 978-1-916938-14-4

Cover designed by Aaron Kent

Edited and Typeset by Aaron Kent

Broken Sleep Books Ltd
PO BOX 102
Llandysul
SA44 9BG

CONTENTS

DID I MENTION?

So I'm in the pub with the rugby lads,
swigging cider and still regretting that bloody Mars bar
I decided to eat for a challenge
(which didn't go down well with the Guinness).
'I hear you do a bit of acting?'
our captain says.
Nice one, Jonathon, I think to myself.
Tell these brick-shouldered,
shower-sharing Spartans that I'm a thespian!
But I've had a drink, and the scrum-half is curious,
so I tell the boys about the plays I've done:
'I once helped to build a barricade,
then fought beside my fellow revolutionaries,
our muskets poised, as bullets sang in our ears.
I've heard war speeches that would put our manly talks
to shame, and make our pre-match huddles
look like an Ann Summers party.
I've dressed a Scottish tyrant in his armour
and informed him of his wife's death,
while he just talked about tomorrows.
At the moment, I'm playing a count...'
'A what?' a prop asks, trying to make a crass pun.
'A *count*,' I repeat, 'in a comedy of manners.
There's nothing like standing on a proscenium stage,
the lights in your eyes as the drapes are opened,
and delivering your lines to an expectant audience.
I've loved acting since I was a boy
with a tail poking out of my arse,

asking Little Red to join her grandma in bed.'

The lads just nod. Some with respect.

Others amazed that their number eight

has been prancing around on stage since childhood.

I take another swig of my pint, smile and say:

'By the way, lads, did I mention that I like to write poetry?'

GERBERA DAISIES

We've got the giggles at a funeral.
The priest keeps getting the name
of the deceased wrong, and my nan
is trying to read the hymnbook upside down:
she doesn't speak Welsh. Here we are:
me, my mother, my aunt,
and my grandmother, shaking
with what looks like grief.
I bite my tongue, hard as I can,
and focus on the coffin. *Come on!*
This is serious! This is death, for God's sake.
I mean, how serious can you get?
But all these suits and muttered prayers
and haleliwias, they're hard
to take seriously. I hope people
aren't so formal when I'm in a box.

A ray of sunlight strikes the stained glass
and illuminates the casket.
The room is silent. Wonderfully silent
now the hymns are finally over.
Afterwards, as we examine
the gerbera daisies and delphiniums,
I smile through fresh tears.

IGLOO

My mother shows me newly developed photos
                 of my father and brother, building an igloo

out of the snow that has fallen so heavy of late.
                They smile like two workmen, happy that they

made something worthwhile. Then I look
            at old photos of family members, their absent smiles.

       Melted snow and twigs on the garden turf.

       All that remains of my father and brother's work.

LEONARD

The house is cold, empty, silent. In the drawers
of an oak dressing table there are coat buttons,
fountain pens and grainy photographs.
I open the mirrored wardrobe and discover
old Christmas presents. Shirts you never wore,
books about football and wars and trains,
the 'Best Grandad' mug I got you last year.
I put the shirts in a plastic charity bag.
There are woolly jumpers, silk handkerchiefs
with embroidered Ls, and the scent of Old Spice.
A pile of neatly folded clothes rests on a chair.
Corded jeans, a leather belt, a navy blue shirt.
I examine the shirt, touch the blood patch
on the collar from when you cut yourself shaving.
I put the pile in another plastic bag and sit
on the cane chair, gaze out of the window
at the soft rain and the dainty hawthorns
in your garden. That view will never pall.

A WEEKEND IN MARCH

I. The Scene

A beam of light breaks through the clouds.
Soon, newlyweds will be framed
next to the fountains, married ears content
with the songs of darting birds in Spring.
Is love a mere affair of weather?
I smoke a cigarette. The light's gone by the time
I'm finished. And now it starts to rain;
leaves rattle as the wind squalls and I struggle
past the museum, suitcase in hand.

II. Joy

Opposite me in the Humanities café
you talk about the grades you got and your
critical theories. I feel emasculated.
I gaze at your leather boots, the gleaming buckles,
watch every word I say, quote Oscar Wilde
when you move on to the subject of marriage.
As you leave, I put my hand in my pocket,
check my manhood is still there, and sigh.

III. Travelling Hopefully

Men marry because they are tired.
My mates must be tired of me.
I get on the coach. I'm free
to make new friends here.
The windows are painted black.

IV. Enemy Arms

On deck, I trace the moon's sad steps.
We'll reach Calais shortly. There are lots
of pretty girls on this trip. I'll be
in a room with seven of them,
like a broken Coriolanus,
finding solace in enemy arms.

V. Hannah

The rain is so heavy it hurts now.
You smile under your green hood. I flirt,
encouraged by bottles of Desperados,
a White Russian, straight shots of vodka.
On the train back, we hold hands,
but once we're in our room again
you're colder than the rain. I sit at the hostel bar,
like Jack Nicholson in *The Shining*. Alone.
'Nobody understands me, Sam!
Je ne parle pas francais, pardon.'

VI. Laila

Laila has me on my knees when she twirls
her velvety hair, lets her looks linger.
This is the last night in Paris and I'm with
the Bristol University girls, drinking at the hostel bar.
Drinking my hangover away. Laila likes
my Welsh accent, even though I say 'pardon'
the French way now. We kiss at the end of the night.
This single life *n'est pas si mal.*

VII. The Score

On the way back to Wales, back to the essays,
back to the friends who bore me with talk
of love and kids and white weddings.
But I've made new friends. Enjoyed myself
with these strangers, feel sorry leaving them.
Leaving her, knowing we'll never speak again.
I look out of the coach window at Welsh words,
shining like diamond glints on snow,
and replay the weekend in my head.
The coach hums a melody as it races down
the long stretch of calm, sunlit road.
It looks as if Spring has finally arrived.

WHAT DAVE THE RAVE SAID

'Times were hard. I mean, I was only a boy.
The sirens would go off and we'd stick
those bloody uncomfortable masks on,
hide in the shelters near St Mary's while
those Nazi bastards dropped bombs
on schools and churches and houses.
It was a difficult childhood. Never knew
my parents. I was brought up by Aunty.
Your grandmother always says that she
was horrible, but she didn't have to raise
me up, and the beatings did no harm.
I've had a good life really, and I've
brought up two beautiful daughters,
but I worry about you all. I really do.
It's a cruel world out there. You hear
about people getting knifed, and all
these hooligans in their hoodies...'

Dave the rave sips his pint of Worthies
and takes a drag of his cigarette:
'Today, the world is full of bastards.'

WHEN YOU HELD MY FINGER

on the night our parents brought you home,
i crept into their room while they slept
so i could take another look at you.

you gazed at me with your blue eyes,
studying my face under the moon,
amazed by the world beyond your cot.

i inhaled your newborn scent, ran my fingers
through your tuft of red hair.
you were tiny, soft as the moonlight.

when you held my finger in your palm
i felt something that i won't feel again,
at least not until i become a dad.

and now, you're nearly as tall as me,
and insist that you have more pubic hair
than i do, even though you're just twelve,

but we've stayed close since you held my finger.

THINE IS THE KINGDOM

And the churchgoers sit in the pews
as the priest tells them to have

      faith.

   I am the resurrection and the life.
   He who believes in me will live,
   even though he dies; and whoever lives
   and believes in me will never die.

And the churchgoers bow their heads.
The dead are silent, without

     prayer.

FACES

When only the moon rages outside my window,
and the room is filled with soundless dark,
I feel my heart thud in my chest and know
that one day this will end, this drumbeat cease
after a sudden blast, or a slow decline.
Wiping sweat from my brow, twisting, turning, toiling,
steeped in memories, I gaze at Adriana,
tell her our first kiss should be to the song,
Pretty Green Eyes. 'But we have brown eyes,' she says.
Caroline smiles as snow begins to fall,
before her taxi arrives, before she leaves me.
Now, I'm with Will, ignorant and happy,
staggering under this same moon, not knowing
he'll find a girl, have kids, and forget that I
was once his friend. Sometimes, without reason,
I fear I won't wake. Better to fall asleep,
distracted by memories, even bittersweet ones,
than watch the future threaten all night, wide-eyed.

COLD DISH

I throw my bag on the floor, rifle
through the questions I received today,

contemplating wild things,
                              like collecting rocks
from the garden and
                    pelting them at you

while you sit at the dinner table, or
                                        stomping on
your fat fiery head.

'Bloody brothers,' I snarl,
as I make my way into the kitchen.

You look up at me, your mouth full
of watermelon, cool water

running down your chin.

You crack a joke and I

just laugh,
            forget what you said earlier.

DEEPLY

In the dream space, intersillient figures cut
through tendrils of smoke, each beat takes on
new meanings, and reality is your audience.
Delivering long, uneven lines, we're all friends,
our issues issuing from us, deeply shallow.
No more problems. Your debit card doesn't serve
its old purpose anymore, and the figures
in the cobalt blue grow ever tantalising.
You battle it out with the hasty clock,
eyes wide, admitting newfound natural light.

Awake. Organs ravaged. Flecks of rain
on the sill. Outside, sober citizens struggling
with their umbrellas, which bloom like black roses.
Alone, frightened, nameless, in a hole,
the figure beside you too obvious, emerged.
And there, brink of despair, you are the audience,
viewing yourself in the harshness of day.

NEW WORLD

We march onwards, my brother and I.
His freckles grow more noticeable,
my skin a darker shade of pink
as sunshine breaks through sinewy clouds.
Cabbage white butterflies mingle
with the falling flecks of blossom
and lemony scents fill our nostrils.
Crashing through the gates of foliage,
our steps quicken at the sound
of oncoming waves, our footprints heavy
on the embroidered ground. We've made it
to the beach, a cool breeze breaking
through the knotted green. The sea
is sighing, soft and gentle,
its fingers playing on the shore's keys.
Aqueous sunlight turns each pebble
into a mirror. Wind-like, we act
as spies, searching for the villain's lair,
hide behind great rocks with carved faces,
stone angels watching the horizon
in immobile guardianship.
A baby seagull, speckled brown,
totters on a stone and then takes
to the air with its older sibling.
Moving past the boulder-heads, we wait
for gunfire, take down some henchmen,
my brother's fiery hair a pyre on shore.
We reach a hollow cave, imagine

that there could be a dragon
exhaling deadly fumes, its eyes
two jewels in a brave new world,
a world where we are valiant heroes.
There are just walls of stone and clay.
I run my hand across the cool surface
and we sit on the ground, wondering what
people would say if they saw us now,
pretending we belonged on screen
or in a book. But there's no intrusion.
Just our ceaseless wonder as we wait
for the lingering sun to set on this.

THAT DAY

We wanted to let Onslow
out of his hutch, so he could play among the daisies
and run across the spiky green grass.
He was given his name by my grampy,
who used to name all our pets, before his own name
was printed in an obituary when I was eighteen.
But Onslow was still. He wouldn't wake up.
No blood. Just stillness. His fur flowing in a faint breeze.
My mum told me he was dead. I couldn't understand.

LEANING ON THE WALL

When I was a child my parents introduced me
to our neighbour, Tony, a round man
with a permanently red nose and a voice
that echoed like the bass notes of a grand piano.
He owned a dog named Bruno, though I used
to call the dog Tony, and Tony Bruno.
We'd spend hours on summer afternoons
talking about dinosaurs (I was known
as Dino Darren, back then) and he soon knew
the difference between a Procompsognathus
and a Velociraptor. He'd always nod and smile,
though I'm not sure if dinosaurs interested him.
We'd stay in our gardens, leaning on the wall,
until the sun sank behind the conifer trees.

Last week, I saw Tony in the Liberal Club
with my dad, and he bought me a pint.
I smiled and called him Bruno, and he asked if
I still wanted to be a palaeontologist. He told me that
his dog had passed away, but Canton life was fine.
My dad sipped his pint, offered condolences
and gazed at the fresh wrinkles on Tony's forehead.
But I just laughed along with Tony, like old times,
feeling that we had an understanding between us
because we'd spent so many hours leaning on the wall.

THE SHRUG

It's 3am. I sit in a smoke-filled room with three friends.
Antonio swaggers in, wearing a thick silver chain,
clinky earrings, everything loud. We watch
Takeshi's Castle and Antonio laughs: 'Look at them,
Chinese bastards. They are very small but clever,
you see. Go back to Japan!' An awkward silence.
'Are you Welsh, my friend?' He turns to me.
'I love the Welsh, very nice people. Respectful.
English are bastards! I am from Amsterdam, my friend.'
'Why don't you like the English?' my mate pipes up.
'I have travelled all over England. The south, not so bad.
But the north is full of bastards. I hate northern English!'
'What's so bad about northern people?' I ask.
Antonio shrugs his shoulders. 'My friend, they are racist.'

OUR FATHER

Mother said you were strange, our father,
when you cursed the children muttering in Mass.

Like the desolate fig tree in the parable you read.

But you were our footy coach, as well as our parish priest,
guarding the changing rooms after a muddy game.

So, when the headmaster told us of the things you'd done,
as the sunlight cascaded behind him,
through the stained glass windows in the school's main hall,

when he told us about the mothers and fathers
and the children you'd tricked,

we muttered and muttered.

We couldn't believe what had come to light that day.

EVER-CHANGING

The world, it passed us by,
ever-changing,
a cyclorama
outside the bus windows,
as I inhaled
honey hair,
gazed at red ringlets,
deep brown eyes.

And then you pressed the fat red button,

leaving me to these
drowsy dreams,
wondering
what your name was, what you did,
a stranger to my world
but not these lines.

SURVIVORS

A green cloud above us, we smoke and laugh
our cares and last night's hangovers away.
Life, frankly, has never seemed so funny.
Penarth beach is a mix of sand and shingle
that stretches below us, as we perch on a cliff top.
The scents of sea air and weed burn our nostrils.
The tide is getting closer. It cuts the beach in half.
The sky grows grey. It'll be evening soon.
'Do you remember last time we got stoned here,
and I persuaded you that island was Majorca!'
My mate, Will, points at some distant flecks of land.
'Yeah, yeah,' I say. 'The tide is coming in fast.
We should make a move.'
'Roll one more up first, mate.'
So, we smoke one more and decide we'll have
our milkshakes and Chilli Sensations in the car.
All we can think about is curing the munchies
as we get off the cliff, using a ladder of rocks
we'd made earlier. We stumble down the beach
and turn a corner. Icy air stifles our laughter.

The tide has reached the top of this part of the beach.
It's lapping against the edge of the cliff
and we don't know any other way out.
'We'll have to climb up the cliff again
to get across,' I tell Will.
But this side of it is too steep. We'd fall to our deaths.
We'll just have to get our feet wet, I suppose.

We've still got the giggles as we tread through the water.
But the waves are hitting us harder than we thought,
and the sea is rising up our bodies now,
smashing us against the base of the cliff.
A wave gives me a wallop and I'm submerged.
I remember what a fortune-teller told my mum:
'Keep your firstborn away from water.'
I raise my head and peer at the sea,
beautiful and terrifying at the same time,
stretching to those ever-distant flecks of land.
I think about the things I haven't achieved
and sob like a child who wants his parents.
You hear about this sort of thing in the news:
fishermen drowning like this.
And that's all Will and I will be remembered as:
two idiotic boys who drowned on Penarth beach.
'Come on!' I shout. I won't let that happen.
I cast my milkshake. It bobs on the water like a gull.
We swim back to shore, gasping for breath,
oblivious to the cramp in our arms and legs.
I want to collapse on the grey pebbles.
But I sprint up the beach, desperate to get away.

Afterwards, we sit in Will's car, drenched.
Somehow, I've managed to save my packet of crisps.
But I can't eat now. I pull my phone from my pocket.
Beep. Beep. A telephonic death rattle.
My wallet, with all my cards in, is soaking.
'Did we just nearly die?' I ask, shivering.
'That was the scariest thing

that has ever happened to me,' Will responds.
Partly ecstatic that we're still alive,
but mainly furious that we were so bloody stupid,
we sit in silence, shaking our heads.
We decide to stay away from each other for a few days.
Like survivors, hoping to forget.

THE FEATHER

Standing in the empty stadium,
my mother looks up at the open roof
and points at a feather falling
through reds and greens. She tells me
a white feather signifies a message
from an angel. 'Your grampy is smiling
at us,' she says. Just as we propitiate
the dead by laying flowers on their graves,
I watch the feather land on cold concrete
and smile without belief, with certain hope.

A TRIP TO MONMOUTH

I hold
these moments
by their stems, let them blossom.
I can see, breathing in this place,
the gothic architecture,
lofty banks,
why poets wrote about
the life of things.
I don't think Shakespeare really visited
The Robin Hood Inn, and I don't know
if I'll ever have the chance to bring
a muse to these beer gardens,
to smoke and drink until
the sky turns red,
knowing faith
is a good thing.
Right now, I savour
the company of my family.
My brother swinging
through the air, parents on the seesaw.
I forget about
the bleak shadows cast
by the vast stonewalls,
the spectres
of mailed knights and monks of folklore.
We get back in the car, the dusty wake
the tail of a ghost in the sunlight.

RAMBLING

Oh I could drink myself into oblivion you know
to stop the thoughts of future
the overwhelming sense of futility
that nobody
will ever know your name
and even this spontaneous scribbling
will never be appreciated.

Those unicorn hopes
die brittle in the mire of myth
and the yellow tang on my breath
dries the tongue that cannot articulate
this purgatorial rambling
all that I haven't begun to explain
even on the brink of oblivion.

HOW FAR WE'VE COME

How far we've come,
travelling years and distances apart,
nothing but unspoken memories
between us now.

                              I saw Will,
pushing a pram in Roath Park.

                              He gazed
at me with sunglass eyes.
A microsecond of acknowledgement.
And then

                              we wafted
through scents
of sprinkled ice creams, green water
and creamy flowers only now blossoming,
planted, like those memories,
a long time ago.
It is hard to reconcile those beaming days
with this enigma of resentment,
those windswept journeys in

                              your car,
those evenings spent with fleckled stars
and lyrics binding

                              us close.
But I find warm comfort in the sight
of these parallel lines with

                              our children,
whose respective names we
can only guess at.

They have all our adventures
to come, all our silliness,
our pig-headedness,
for which we'll scorn them
as if we were perfect texts.
I guess we need characters for different scenes,
and though ours have clouded
they made us who we are.
Crunching acorns, holding tiny hands,
I'm sure you too can see just how far we've come.

EULOGY

You loved stories.
Whenever I visited, you'd always have
a fresh book next to your armchair.
And you were a storyteller yourself.
Anecdotes from your childhood
would shed laughter.
In your armchair,
you were a real sit-down comedian.

In the story of our lives,
you played several characters:
grandmother,
mother-in-law,
mother,
wife.

So long as I've known you and granddad,
you'd bicker like the Twits.
But often—especially if one of you
was hurt or unwell—translucent affection
could be discerned.

I remember you
standing up to bullies on the bus
when picking me up from school,
holding you back when some yobs
barged into a shop in Canton
and started threatening the staff:

I see you now, poised
behind a stall with a frying pan
clenched in your fist.

I dance up and down
the living room with you.
You don't complain
as we watch *Jurassic Park*
and I say all the lines
before any of the actors.

The wild woman of many
a Christmas and New Year party.
The woman who nestled my dreams.
This is a chapter we wish hadn't been written.
Amidst the thunder of prayer
we are told to celebrate life.
That's hard to accept right now.
But we owe the memory-makers
our laughter.
To keep telling your story.

DAPHNE DU MAURIER

Rummaging through
my late grandmother's closet,
I pull out a copy
of Daphne du Maurier's *Rebecca*,
leaf through the foxed pages.
Some of the corners show signs
of having been folded over.
I imagine her reading it
in another life,
leaving traces of herself
in the withered spine,
in the faded letters.
Books aren't just gateways
to other worlds;
they are material objects,
retaining ghostly wisps and whispers,
inerasable evidence from the past.
I tell my class so when I teach this book.
They shake their heads.
But I have seen ghosts too
gliding among the throngs
of those fresh-faced students.

PONTYPRIDD KARAOKE LADY

Ponytpridd karaoke lady
her children and husband
make up the audience
in the front row

she sings
to these ears pricked
the distracted
hubbub half-decent
by burbled lyrics of yore

she floats
in that moment
as intoxicated palms
beat her way back

and she looks
at her fans
away acrid smoke
those in the front row
and imagines a life
feels she lost willingly

STICKY STATUES

Visiting my grandfather's friend

                          my little fingers

reached for a bust.

He said:

                          don't touch that!

Your hand will stick forever.

And I'm ashamed to say

                          most of childhood I thought

all statues were sticky.

SYLVESTER STALLONE

Cuddling in your bed.
On a few occasions
you've said the words
jokingly.
But I don't probe.
Want the moment to be real.
Breath warm against my skin.
Fresh ginger, creamy sandalwood
make nostrils flare.
I'll never get used to your eyes.
Happy and hazel.
Want to say those words.
Silence.
So much to be spoken.
Acknowledgement.
Closer than ever before.
But the moment passes.
My creative writing tutor
has warned me:
avoid that abstract noun
if possible.
Maybe that's why I struggle.
'I love you yeah yeah yeah...'
You paraphrase a song.
'That's a funny way of telling me.'
A grin, I twine fingers in yours.
'But I *do* love you,' you say.
'I love you...' I repeat those words,
muffled by your blanket.
Sound like Sylvester Stallone
as Rocky Balboa.

ON FATHERHOOD

Like that shepherd exploring
the topography of grief,
I met your vast eyes, sins of youth
yet committed, an ocean of blue
washing over me and your mother,
as we breathed in your forehead
and you probed our napes
with the grains of your nails.
Once intangible, a lock from a dream,
in moments I knew I would sleep
for you, and as your hair sprouted
and you blossomed in a bed
of ardent love, of blessed care,
we relived our childhoods
contemplating your wooden stage.
And sometimes old photos of me
make me take double, thick-haired, blond,
the red splash that you share,
a staff in your grip, raising fossils.
And sometimes I smile a tomb,
a Centurion servant, when you replay
the scenes I shared with the boy
who now shares your name,
like when you first tricked and treated.
And I remember those evenings
when we were kids, holes for arms
and heads in bin bags.
You stir life in the wilted,

my son come into the world
to relume the darkness we stumbled.
In your daylight we play again.

ACKNOWLEDGEMENTS

LAY OUT YOUR UNREST

Milton Keynes UK
Ingram Content Group UK Ltd.
UKHW041958160324
439502UK00004B/118

9 781916 938144